US & THEM

WHAT THE BRITISH THINK

OF THE AMERICANS

PAUL DAVIS

Published in 2004 by Laurence King Publishing Ltd
71 Great Russell Street
London WC1B 3BP
United Kingdom
Tel: +44 20 7430 8850
Fax: +44 20 7430 8880
e-mail: enquiries@laurenceking.co.uk
www.laurenceking.co.uk

A catalogue record for this book is available from the British Library.

ISBN 1 85669 398 8

Printed in China

Acknowledgements
Thanks go to Laurence King, Jo Lightfoot, Harry Ritchie, Judi Krant, Jonathan
Ellery, Stefan Pietsch, Chateau Marmont Hotel.

This book is dedicated to Christina Morassi for all her help and support.

Foreword

It all started when I was visiting San Francisco with my good friend Callum. We decided to cross America to the Atlantic coast on a motorcycle (two up, so you can imagine the pain after over 4,000 miles). That trip is where my fascination with the USA really took off. I've been back many times since then and noticed that my drawings and writings began to form the idea of what we think of each other's cultures, habits and character (after all, we're supposed to have this so-called 'special relationship'). So I asked hundreds of people from both sides of the Atlantic 'Excuse me, what do you think of the British/Americans?'. What follows are true quotes from real people. Some of the drawings are based on photographs and video tape I shot as it's difficult to talk, listen, write and draw all at the same time. But the veracity should be evident because it's impossible to make this stuff up.

Paul Davis

Paul Davis is an artist and illustrator, based in London.

Introduction

Mundanely, if you must, this book is a record of one man's encounters with passers-by in Britain and America. He asked them, because he wanted to ask them something, what they thought about each other's countries.

It's not as if this was a trick question, or even a tricky one, worth £250,000 on *Millionaire*. Britons might reasonably be expected to have some cogent thoughts about the world's only superpower. Equally, it's not outrageous to expect that American citizens could have an interesting reflection or two about the country which used to own it and which has been its staunchest/most slavish ally.

But no.

There are two plausible explanations for this. The first is that the samplees were wondering what the hell was going on with this strange, thin man who'd got talking to them as they were sitting at the bar, minding their own business, or just come up to them in the street and suddenly here he was, this strange, thin man, request-ing their thoughts to be wrenched away – from the Heineken they were nursing or the dairy products they were putting in their trolley, the escapade they were trying to recall or the bereavement they were enduring – and abruptly turned to the issue of transatlantic cultural perceptions. The second explanation is that almost every-body, with some exceptions such as me and you, has a head full of mince. 'Q: What do you think about Britain? A: Oh, I don't know about that. My wife here is an anti-capitalist "feeling" therapist who works a lot within the business community.'

Consistent as this book is in revealing the daftness, knee-jerk hostility, bigotry, fearful suspicion and, above all else, the barking solipsism of normal adults whose only shared feature is that they were once bumped into by Paul Davis, there is a difference between the two halves of the book in the nature of the daftness, knee-jerk hostility, etc. Facile, skewed, strange, irretrievably prejudiced, immune from sensible reflection – British opinions about Americans are, evidently, all of these and more.

But, however inadequate or deranged, they are at least based on some sort of knowledge. It's simply not possible for Brits – or anyone else in the world with access to a television – to remain unaware of the USA, just as they can't be unaware of the weather. Some/most/all of the British samplees obviously command little/no considered expertise on the subject, but you don't have to have a degree in meteorology to know what it feels like to be caught in the rain.

The absence of complete and utter ignorance cannot be said of the American contributors. 'The Queen, fog, tea' – it's got to the point where a Brit can read that and feel not just dismay, frustration and resentment but also relief and gratitude. (Three! And they're all accurate!) 'Cowboy hats, George Bush, not giving a shit about the rest of the world' would be an equivalent list because its insularity is one of the defining features of American society. 'Q: What do you think about Britain? A: It's so kinda like I dunno.' If the eventual downfall of the Roman empire could have been predicted by an onlooker at a slave-serviced debauch, then we can see in the prevailing lackadaisical ignorance one possible reason why the USA won't dominate the world for ever.

And it won't. An empire's life-span is, what, 200 years? 400, tops. So it is likely that the USA's global dominance will be superseded some time this century – by China maybe, or a supranational global marketplace, or New Zealand after the third world war or some virus.

If Americans want to know what it will feel like after their empire falls, what their country will be like after it's no longer number one, they can best approach time-travel by applying for a passport and flying to Britain. That's what the USA will be like – a bit run-down, a bit old-fashioned, with a token seat on the Security Council and an accent the Chinese just love. And if that seems silly, let's remember that only a century ago the *New York Times* declared that the British empire was obviously invincible.

It's because both Britain and America have been the most powerful countries in the world for the last two centuries that both countries are resented, and with similar results. Along with the inscrutable Japanese, the humourless Germans and the suicidal Swedes, Brits and Yanks take their places in the cartoon world of stereotypes as large and loud, arrogant and stupid – triangularly obese midwesterners and wardrobe-sized hooligans, know-nothing loudmouths and brain toffs, all monoglot xenophobes with a penchant for military violence.

If that doesn't seem at all fair, if that kind of glib generalization seems hurtful and just plain *wrong*, nearly *racist* in fact in the way it blithely ignores an uncountable number of complexities and virtues, then I'm afraid you're going to have to brace yourself for what follows, as one strange, thin man files his dispatches from the front-line of ordinary human absurdity.

Harry Ritchie

Harry Ritchie was born in Kirkcaldy, Fife, Scotland in 1958.
He is the author of four books, most recently the novel 'Friday Night Club'.
He lives in London.

THE AMERICANS
ARE JOLLY NICE
PEOPLE. A LITTLE
EXTREME AT
TIMES — YOU
KNOW, ALL THE
MURDERING AND
INSIDER TRADING
AND THE LIKE,
BUT I GENUINLEY
LIKE 'EM.
APART FROM
THAT BLOODY
MADONNA
WHO'S REALLY
BEGINNING
TO PUSH
HER LUCK,
I CAN TELL
YOU, I MEA

THE PEOPLE ARE VERY MUCH UNDERRATED

The Americans are SO easy to laugh at. Especially those silly tourists.
MWAAH-HAW!
ABBEY NATIONAL

IT MUST BE KIND OF GOOD
NOT TO GIVE A SHIT ABOUT
THE REST OF THE WORLD

IT AMAZES ME HOW ~~THE~~
FANTASTIC THEIR STREET CLEANERS,
COPS etc LOOK. BRITAIN? SWEAT-BOX
UNFASHIONABILITY.

THEY'RE FEARFULLY
OVER-CONFIDENT BASED
ON PROFOUND PARANOIA.

THEY ARE NOTHING BUT EVIL

THEY ENGULF US. BUT I KNOW THEY'RE
ALL PARANOID, VAIN & INSECURE.

well, I have tons
of Yank chums and on
the whole, they're all O.K.
Don't drink much, mind.

LIVERPOOL

6% HAVE PASSPORTS

70% HAVE BEEN TO
DISNEYWORLD OR DISNEY-
LAND.

THEY ARE LIKE
CHILDREN.

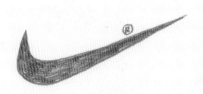

SUPER, MEGA, BIG MACS, STARBUCKS.
I MEAN, TALL, GRANDE, VENTI IS
TOTAL BOLLOCKS. WHY
NOT SMALL, MEDIUM,
LARGE? BRITAIN FOLLOWS
THEIR SPURIOUS IDEALS.
AS USUAL. DOES THIS MAKE
SENSE? SORRY. SOME OF
THEM ARE NICE. GOD,
I MUST SOUND AWFUL.
ER... PLEASE DON'T
PUT THIS IN.

STOP GOING ON ABOUT IT.
I'M POORLY.

YOU HAVE THE NEW YORK PEOPLE
AND THE L.A. PEOPLE, AND THE REST
ARE ONE BIG HERD.

I CAN'T THINK ABOUT THAT KIND OF THING, I'M AFRAID. ONE REALLY SHOULDN'T JUDGE

HOW COME THEIR CHEERLEADERS ARE EVER SO SLIGHTLY CHUBBY?

london E8

YOU ASKED ME
THIS THE OTHER
DAY, AND LIKE I TOLD
YOU — I DON'T KNOW

YOU WATCH A BIG HERD OF BUFFALO. THE ONE
AT THE FRONT BEGINS TO CROSS THE RIVER.
IT'S HALF-WAY ACROSS AND THE OTHERS
FOLLOW. THEN YOU KNOW THEY'RE IN TROUBLE.
THAT'S WHAT I THINK OF AMERICA.

BEST NOT TO THINK ABOUT MIDDLE AMERICA
BECAUSE THE HORROR IS TOO GREAT.

THE AMERICANS
ARE A BUNCH
OF TERRIFYING
CHRISTIAN
FUNDAMENTAL-
ISTS. ▓▓
APART FROM
THE MILITANT
ISLAMICS.
AND THE
WEIRD MORMONS.
OH, AND THE
SURVIVALISTS.
FUCKING FUCKED UP.
SCARES ME.

I'M THE BASTARD CHILD OF
SOME G.I. FROM THE SECOND
WORLD WAR. MY MUM WON'T REALLY
TALK ABOUT IT. I DON'T CARE. NEVER
BEEN THERE.
NEVER WILL.

THE U.S. SNEEZES AND THE U.K. CATCHES A COLD. OR PNEU- -MONIA.

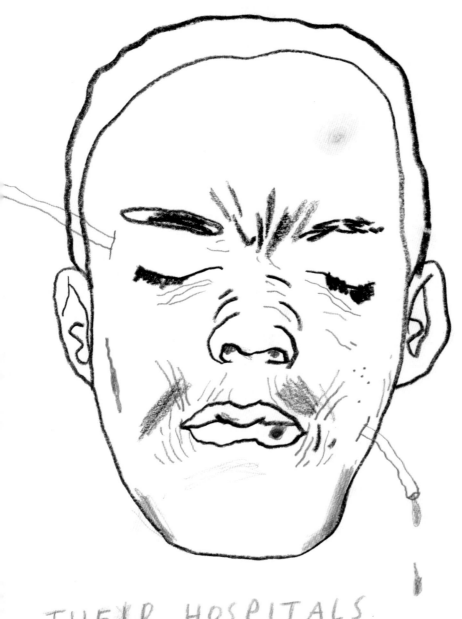

THEIR HOSPITALS
ARE BETTER — MEDICARE AND
ALL THAT

MEMO

AWESOME THIS, AWESOME
THAT, STARBUCKS, FUCKING
MCDONALDS.

THEY DON'T GIVE ASHIT.

I Think the majority of
Americans are lonely people,
It's the companies that
feed them crap that
worries me. I suppose it's
their decision. Short run
becomes long
run.

EXCEL
HOTEL TOKYU
G TOKYU HOTELS

AWESOME THIS,
AWESOME THAT.
WHY IS EVERYTHING
SO AWE-
SOME?
IT ISN'T,
IS IT?

The babes are,
are, are bloody
marvellous.
Bloody marvellous.
shagged one
once. Not
bad!

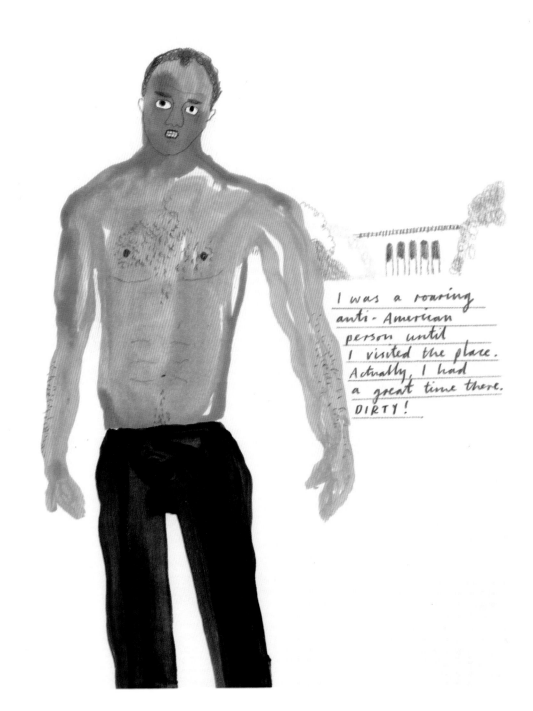

I was a roaring anti-American person until I visited the place. Actually, I had a great time there. DIRTY!

THE WAY THEY PUT
CHICKEN, BEEF, FISH AND
CHEESE TOGETHER IS
MORE THAN WE NEED

I'VE FORGOTTON. I DEALT
WITH PEOPLE, NOT AMERICANS. BUT
IT IS THE UNHAPPIEST COUNTRY
I'VE VISITED.

THEY WANT TO BE AN EMPIRE LIKE
WE WERE. IT'LL NEVER HAPPEN.
YOU GOT YOUR ROMANS, TURKS, US.
MIND YOU, THEY'VE GOT HAWAII. AND
I'D SOONER BE WITH THE STATES THAN
                              EUROPE.

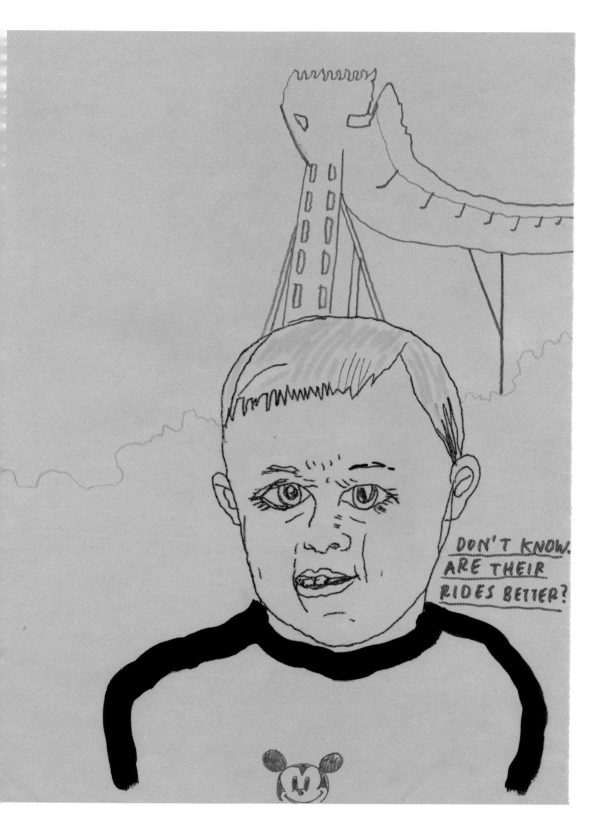

AMERICAN CONCEPTUAL ARTISTS SEEM MORE CONCEPTUAL THAN THEIR BRITISH COUNTERPARTS. BUT I COULD BE LYING AS AN ART-FORM.

HMM — I DON'T REALLY
KNOW I'M AFRAID. ALL
I DO KNOW IS SAINTS HAVE
A GOOD AND UPSTANDING PAST
AND THE SINNERS OF THIS
WORLD FACE A
TERRIBLE FUTURE.

I'M OFTEN PLEASANTLY SURPRISED BY THE INDIVIDUAL AMERICANS I HAVE MET. THEY ▲ WERE GREAT.

I STRUGGLE WITH THEM.
I HAVE A FRIEND — WELL NOT A FRIEND —
I HATE HIM ACTUALLY. IT'S THE
GOD THING
THAT'S SO
ANNOY-
ING.

he thinks
he's better
than anyone
else who doesn't
believe. Prick.

The Americans?
Well, they seem
to lone it that
they're YANKS

I MET LOTS WHEN I WAS
WORKING THERE. NEVER TALKED
ABOUT POLITICS, NEVER ABOUT THE
WORLD, NONE OF THEM VOTED.

MMMM - APART FROM
JUSTIN TIMBERLAKE -
WE'RE ALL FUNDAMENTALLY
THE SAME, SHARING THE
PRETTY MUCH SAME IDEALS,
DESIRES AND NEEDS.
BORING QUESTION ACTUALLY...

Claridge's

I beg your
paan?

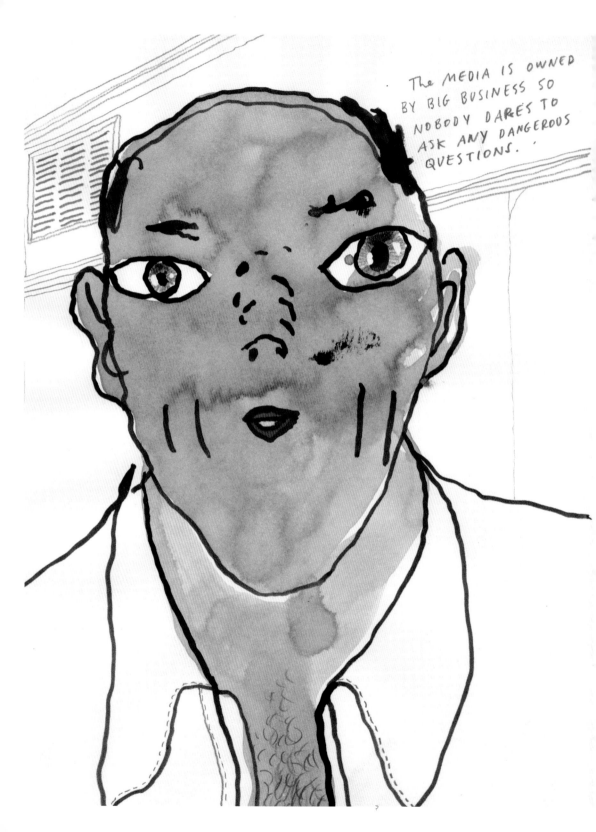

CENTRAL RESERVATIONS

Leeds
BY THE STATION

WHAT'S THE POINT

IN ASKING ME

THAT?

IT'S HERE WITH DE VERE

DE VERE HOTELS
Hotels of character, run with pride

BASTARDS

SUCKERS

REMEMBER : I'M AN
AMERICAN SO I CAN'T
JUDGE.

THE ENGLISH?
I LIKE THEM—
EXCEPT THAT MY
BOSS IS ENGLISH.
WHO'S AN
ASSHOLE.

Same as Japan, right?
Real polite.

5th & SUNSET

YOU SOUND LIKE
A BUNCH
OF FUCKING SNOBS,
MAN.

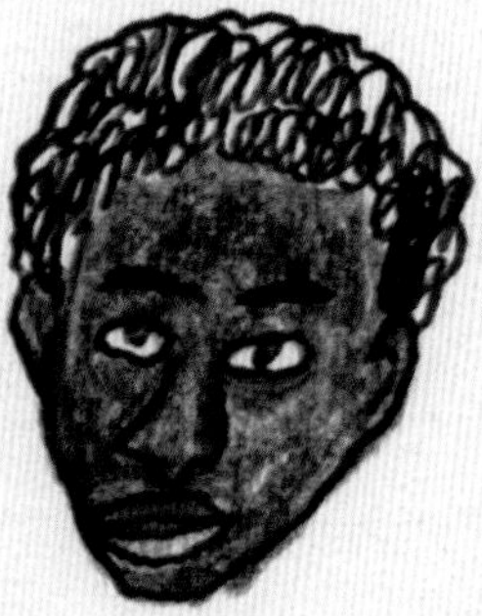

I don't have a problem with it.

Alarming, I'd say. Gives us something
to shoot at.

New York is full of fools. Assholes.
I'd never live there.

I don't know — Ahm a loveable cuss.

N.O.: Yeah the Brits were here 250 years
ago. Won't forget that in a hurry.

"Beatles."

"No. Rolling Stones"

"They're ugly"

"Yeah. True"

"Beatles were the most homely"

"True! Where are they now?"

"True!"

~~Eat~~ Trying to take the elevator to the
top floor.

YOU GUYS HAVE
SHITTY TEETH

AM I GETTING
PAID FOR THIS?

what to you think
about the British?

I don't

know, it's a

tricky question

to answer when

you don't

never think about

it . . .

"I GOTTA SAY, THE ENGLISH
DON'T BREED LOOKERS.
NO OFFENCE." (CHATEAU MARMONT)

The family education is totally great.

The DRINKER SAYS:

IRAQ? WELL I KNOW EL PASO. IT'S ROUGH.
AIRBASE. WHORE HOUSES. WILD
FRONTIER TIME. I WAS WITH THIS
GIRL. SOLDIERS IN
A JEEP. FLASHING
THEIR GUNS SHOUTING
"WE'RE GONNA
KILL YOUR GIRL-
FRIEND. AND
THEN RAPE
HER." OR WAS
IT THE OTHER
WAY ROUND?
DISTURBING.
THEY'RE
SUPPOSED
TO PROTECT
US.

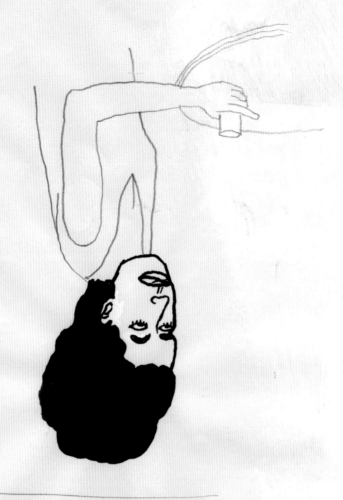

ENGLAND?
ONE CROWDED HOUR
OF GLORIOUS LIFE,
I DON'T KNOW.

I GOT A KICK OUT OF FAWLTY TOWERS.
IT WAS REAL ARISTOCRATIC.

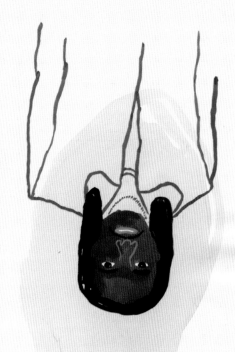

LITTLE SNOBBY,
LITTLE HIGH MAINTENANCE

I'M GOING OUT WITH ONE, DUDE.

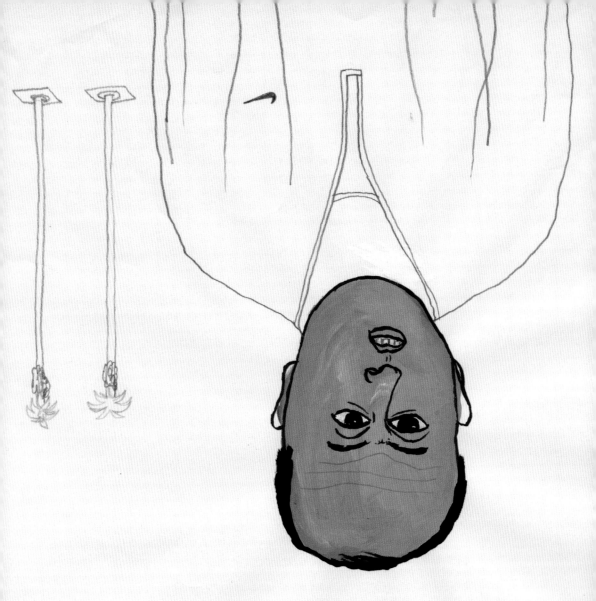

THE RACES ARE SO MUCH MORE
POLARIZED HERE — I MEAN WHEN
YOU WALK AROUND ENGLAND, ASIANS,
BLACKS, EVERYONE KIND OF MIXES
TOGETHER

Honour my ~~Prejudice~~ prejudice

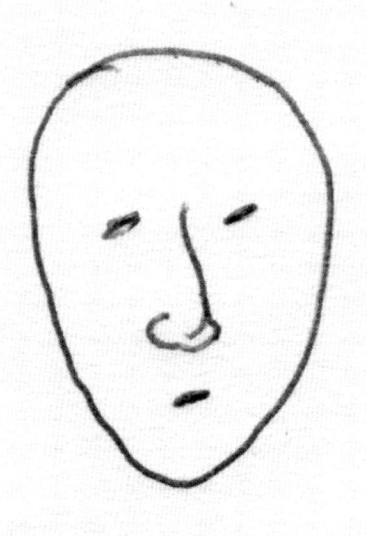

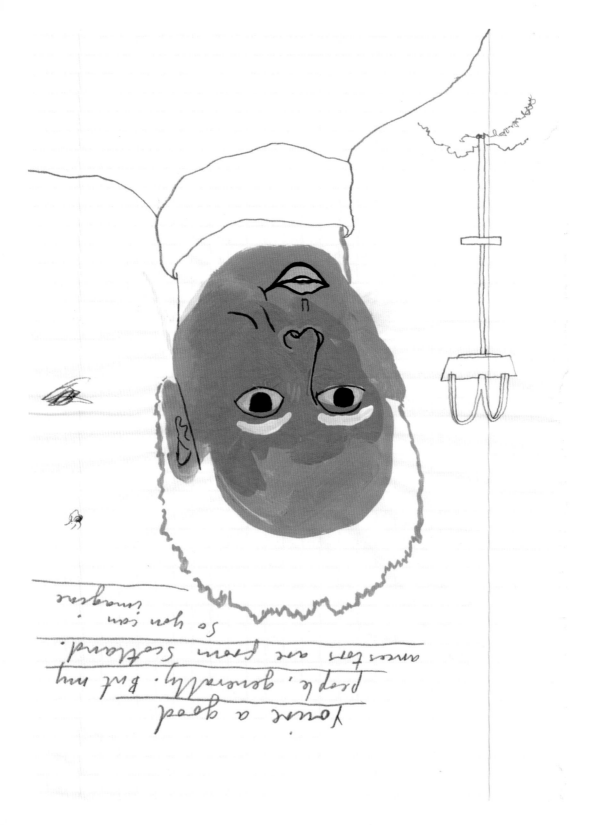

You're a good people, generally. But my ancestors are from Scotland. So you can commiserate.

X 1,000,000

LOVE YOUR ACCENT.

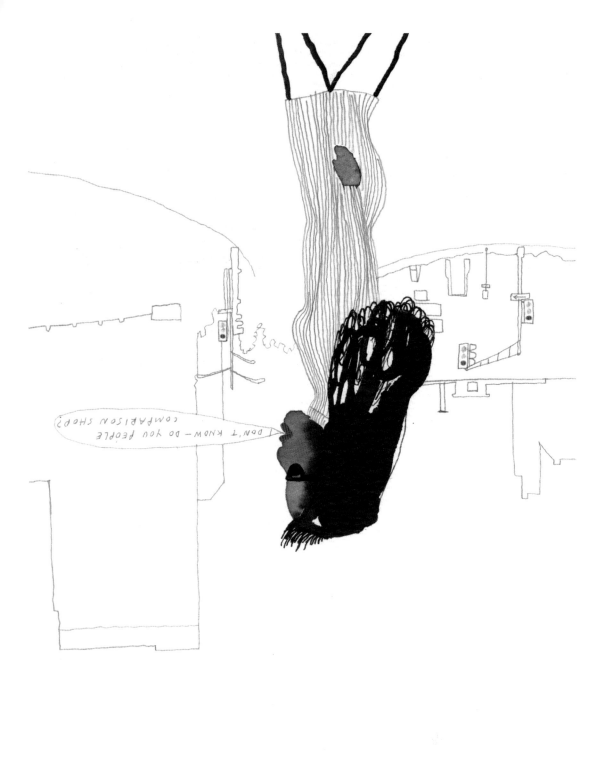

"WELL, I DON'T KNOW ABOUT THAT.
SEE, I'M FROM NORTH DAKOTA AND, YOU
KNOW, THERE WERE FOREIGN FILMS
THAT WERE MADE AVAILABLE, SO YOU KNOW,

I'M NOT SURE ... IT'S DIFFICULT,
THERE'S NOTHING WRONG WITH THAT TYPE OF
THING — WE'RE PRETTY SOPHISTICATED, SO
YOU KNOW, TO WHAT KIND OF ... "
"I ASKED YOU YOU'RE THOUGHTS ON BRITAIN."
"They're snobbish."

FINE UPSTANDING CHRISTIAN PEOPLE
ARE THE ONES I'VE MET, I WAS IN
BIRMINGHAM IN THE MID LANDS.
BEAUTIFUL TIME, ALTHOUGH IT RAINED SOME.

CATRINA

MAN, THE ENGLISH ARE
A GREAT PEOPLE. ESPECIALLY
THE MARINES. I'VE BEEN LUCKY,
I'VE BEEN TO NORWAY, DENMARK
.... VIETNAM .... KOREA......

1776, YOU BULLISH, COLONIAL HAS-BEENS

WHAAAT? YOUR ASKING THE WRONG PERSON HERE.
I SEE NO BARRIERS WITH PEOPLE.   OK, FINE, THEN.
EVERYONE'S THE SAME.
I'VE NEVER BEEN OUT OF
L.A. BORN AND BRED

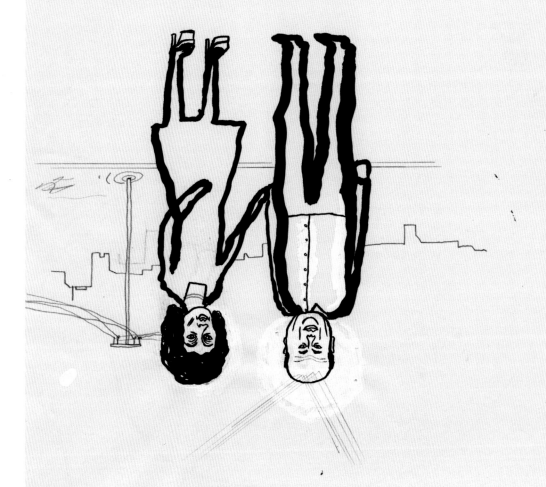

CHICAGO

Y'ALL ARE FINE.
LOVE YOOR ACCENTS
LOVE YOOR ROYALS.

FUCKING ENGLISH
PUSSY? WHOA!

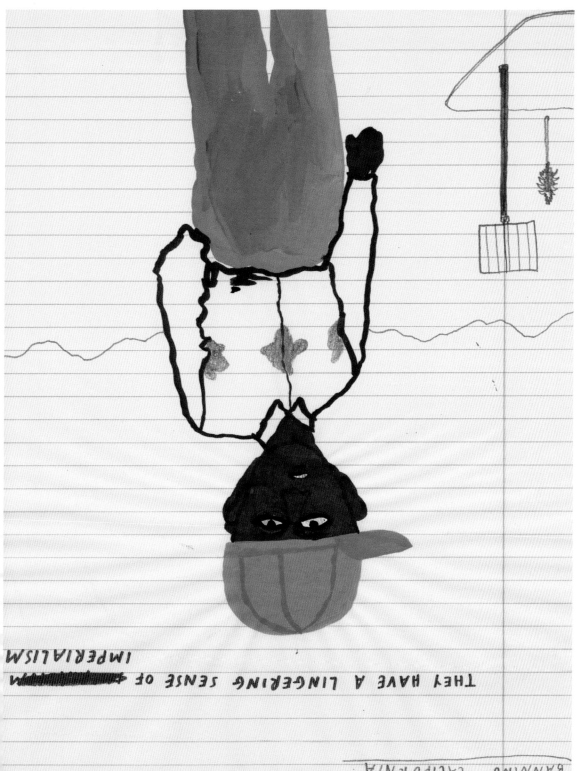

THEY HAVE A LINGERING SENSE OF IMPERIALISM

BANNING - CALIFORNIA

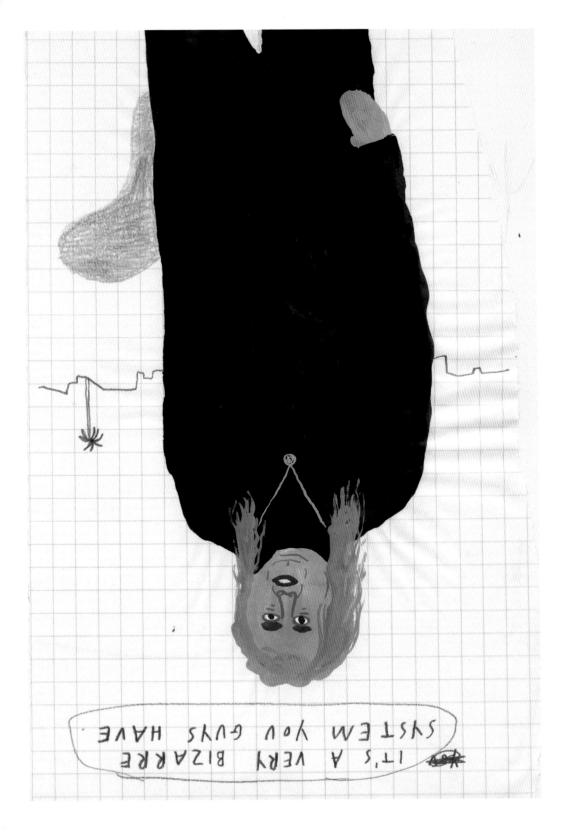

IT'S A VERY BIZARRE
SYSTEM YOU GUYS HAVE.

BLAIR'S
OUR ONLY
ALLY AND
I WANT TO
THANK YOU
- GUYS -

YOU ENGLISH ARE OK — YOU KNOW THE FRENCH
AND RUSSIANS? THOSE PEOPLE ARE LIKE
FUCKING VENDING MACHINES

CHICAGO
HOTEL

There's a certain 'Old School'
arrogance.
AH HATE IT!

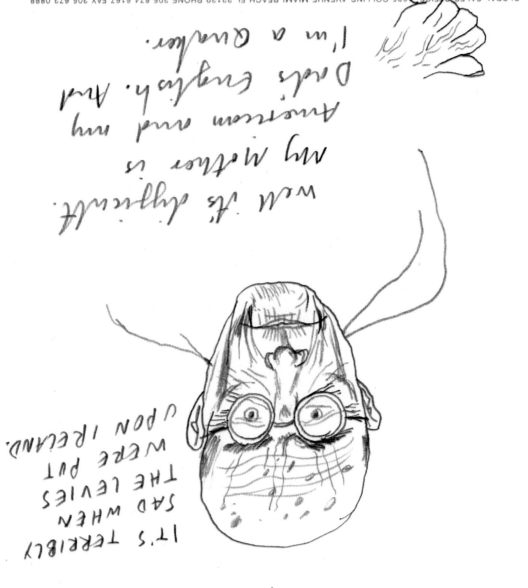

Well it's difficult. My Mother is American and my Dad's English. And I'm a Quaker.

IT'S TERRIBLY SAD WHEN THE LEVIES WERE PUT UPON IRELAND.

NATHAN CLARKE

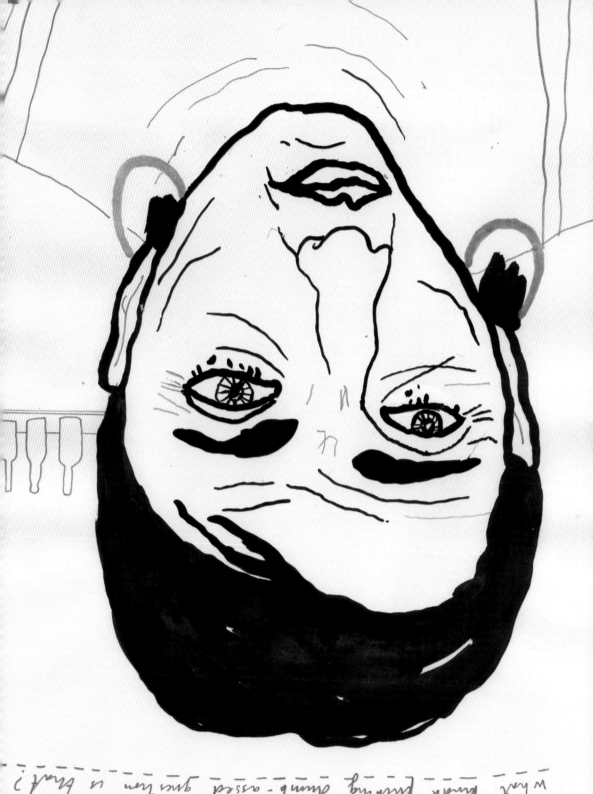

What kind fucking dumb-assed question is that?

IT'S SO KINDA LIKE I DUNNO.

OH, FOREFATHERS, FORMAL, SNOBBISH, PROPER.

YOU GUYS GET ON MY NERVES

DAVIS

"EXCUSE ME."

"YEAH?"

"GOT A MINUTE?"

"YEAH."

"COULD I ASK YOU A QUESTION?"

"SURE, GO AHEAD."

"UM, WHAT DO THE BRITS OR BRITAIN MEAN TO YOU?"

"I'M NOT QUALIFIED TO ANSWER THAT
BECAUSE I DON'T KNOW ANY."

"THANKS".

"NO PROBLEM"

"WOULD YOU LIKE A DRINK?"

"NO THANKS, I'M FINE."

"OK — BYE THEN."

"YEAH."

IT'S LIKE, TOTALLY
MYSTERIOUS

LOVE ENGLISH MEN. EXCEPT WHEN THEY'RE
A LITTLE BIT PIGGISH AT SOCCER GAMES

they're such a civilized people,
what they say is really, really smart.
Americans are just fucking stupid
and I can say that because (a)
I'm American and (b) I'm stupid.

Her name is KISSY

NOWADAYS WE SHARE A COMMON
LANGUAGE, COMMON AIMS.
CULTURE IS ALMOST SHARED
BETWEEN US EXCEPT FOR THE PAINFUL
FACT FOR YOU GUYS IS THAT WE JUST
ABOUT RULE THE PLANET. WHAT DO YOU SAY
ABOUT THAT? I MEAN, DON'T GET ME WRONG—
I LOVE THE BRITS— BUT, YOU KNOW, WE KICK ASS.

In this book, Paul warmed my proud, capitalist, anti-perspirant wearing American heart. He bridges the gaps by exposing our parallels. He showed me that Americans and British share more than the blood on our hands and *Who Wants to be a Millionaire?*

We're both deflated imperialists, lacing up our trendy trainers one foot at a time, scrambling for swag.

Thank you, Paul, for drawing your funny drawings instead of taking the mood-stabilizing medicine you so clearly need. (High-five, dude.)

Judith Krant

Judith Krant is an actor/writer/director based in New York and Los Angeles. She has directed television commercials, and is currently writing a script for a feature film.

He's back on his side of the pond. He had his joyride and was ready to go back to his Twingo, a car that would be laughed off the road in these parts. We don't drive cars that use bicycle tires. It's just not safe when you have to contend with seven lanes of Turbo-charged SUVs (high-five!!).

Now here comes Paul, illuminating what's lurking behind the myth of our glossy façades: goofballs grasping to connect through designer logos and pop culture sound bites. Reading the dialogue, I realized you English are not all that different from us Americans. You aren't smarter or more clever (like I always thought). You're just less tan. You are The Beatles. We are Elvis. You are Marmite. We are Miracle Whip. You are Guy Ritchie. We are Madonna. You are PG Tips. We are Coke. You are Boiled. We are Deep-fried.

But more importantly: You are Beer. We are Beer.

Paul is a paper and pen documentarian. He delivers something timeless and interactive. The intrigue is in what he chooses to show us, and what he chooses to leave out. Every drawing is layered with stories, starting with the random pieces of paper that are Paul's canvases. They remain like a journal, spontaneous and urgent. It's the world seen through the eyes of someone incessant, diabolical and pure.

Everyone seems to be awkwardly floating in Paul's stripped-down, horizon-less worlds. His graphic economy renders each of us in a field of profound isolation. Herein lies the complexity of Paul's work. The edges left empty: we hover in a world searching for context. Whether you're Prince Charles at a polo match or a babe on stage in a wet t-shirt contest, we're all heaving through the muggy hollow between others and ourselves. Alone together.

Introduction

Two people across the hall just high-fived each other. It's what we're about over here: high-fiving. We're high-fiving so much, the truth is, we don't think about you Brits much at all. Unless it's to remind you of 1776 (gimme-five!).

We're young. We can't help it. We're globe toddlers. You're only on our radar in broad strokes. I mean, sure, if one of us is confronted by a Brit, especially some tsunami of a man like Paul, we'll cook up a good answer. We'll compliment the accent. Reference our favorite Monty Python or Benny Hill spoof. Commiserate about Diana. Mention a friend we had who was one of you. But know this: when we are alone, amongst ourselves, we don't talk about y'all at all.

You guys, on the other hand, don't seem like high-fivers. You're all so polite and reserved. Wouldn't be well-mannered to let your ego swell and peak to a high-five. Even your rough-and-tumble rugby team refrains from a pre-game chant.

I had an English lover, so I know all about it. He came out to LA to make his fortune with the skills he learned in London. People were ooh-ing and aah-ing over his accent everywhere we went.

First thing he did was buy an American car. A big '80s convertible Caddie El Dorado. So what if it only got nine miles to the gallon? He was pimpin.' Even Snoop Dogg gave him props for the thing. (True, I swear.) He was so damn happy with it, the second thing he did was to buy another American car. A '70s muscle car right out of some car chase in *Starsky and Hutch*. But he was terrified of speed. It just wasn't in his nature to move fast, I guess.

Highways made him terribly nervous. He'd be white-knuckling the steering wheel; telling me not to talk while he was driving. I hate to see a good machine wasted on a timid operator, so eventually I took over the wheel. He liked the passenger seat. A lot. Too much.

Foreword

It all started when I was visiting San Francisco with my good friend Callum. We decided to cross America to the Atlantic coast on a motorcycle (two up, so you can imagine the pain after over 4,000 miles). That trip is where my fascination with the USA really took off. I've been back many times since then and noticed that my drawings and writings began to form the idea of what we think of each other's cultures, habits and character (after all, we're supposed to have this so-called 'special relationship'). So I asked hundreds of people from both sides of the Atlantic 'Excuse me, what do you think of the British/Americans?'. What follows are true quotes from real people. Some of the drawings are based on photographs and video tape I shot as it's difficult to talk, listen, write and draw all at the same time. But the veracity should be evident because it's impossible to make this stuff up.

Paul Davis

Paul Davis is an artist and illustrator, based in London.

LAURENCE KING

Published in 2004 by Laurence King Publishing Ltd
71 Great Russell Street
London WC1B 3BP
United Kingdom
Tel: +44 20 7430 8850
Fax: +44 20 7430 8880
e-mail: enquiries@laurenceking.co.uk
www.laurenceking.co.uk

A catalogue record for this book is available from the British Library.

ISBN 1 85669 398 8

Printed in China

Acknowledgements
Thanks go to Laurence King, Jo Lightfoot, Harry Ritchie, Judi Krant, Jonathan Ellery, Stefan Pietsch, Chateau Marmont Hotel.

This book is dedicated to Christina Morassi for all her help and support.

US & THEM

WHAT THE AMERICANS THINK OF THE BRITISH

PAUL DAVIS